HISTORY UNCUT

THE REAL
Albert Einstein

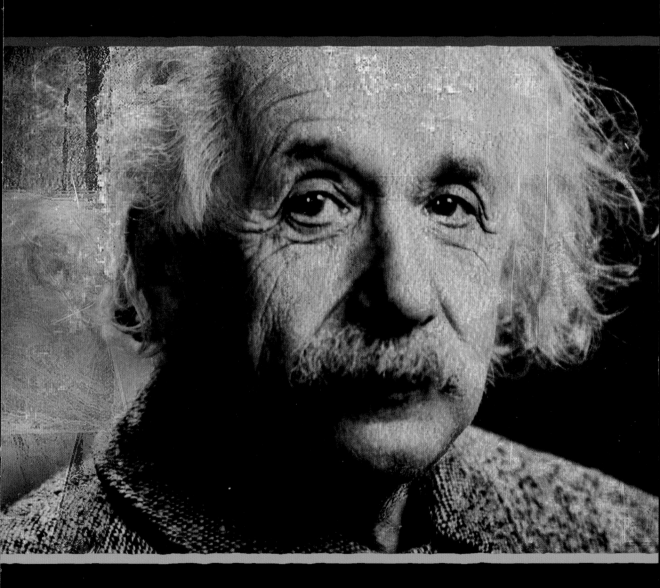

Virginia Loh-Hagan

45th Parallel Press

Published in the United States of America by Cherry Lake Publishing
Ann Arbor, Michigan
www.cherrylakepublishing.com

Reading Adviser: Marla Conn MS, Ed., Literacy specialist, Read-Ability, Inc.
Book Designer: Felicia Macheske

Photo Credits: © Turner, Orren Jack, photographer. Albert Einstein, -1955. , ca. 1947. Photograph. Retrieved from the Library of Congress, https://www.loc.gov/item/2004671908, cover; 1; Library of Congress, Prints & Photographs Division, photograph by Harris & Ewing, [reproduction number, e.g., LC-USZ62-123456] 5, 30; © Alberto Andrei Rosu/Shutterstock.com, 7; © arrowsmith2/Shutterstock.com, 9; © Everett Historical/ Shutterstock.com, 11, 12, 17; © Alvovl/Shutterstock.com, 15; ETH-Bibliothek Zürich, Bildarchiv / Fotograf: Unbekannt / Portr_03106 / Public Domain Mark, 19; Library of Congress, Prints & Photographs Division, photograph by Harris & Ewing, [reproduction number, e.g., LC-USZ62-123456], 20; © Vyntage Visuals/Shutterstock.com, 23; © Gajus/Shutterstock.com, 24; © Viktor Gladkov/Shutterstock.com, 27; © Thanakrit Sathavornmanee/ Shutterstock.com, 29

Graphic Elements Throughout: © iulias/Shutterstock.com; © Thinglass/Shutterstock.com; © kzww/Shutterstock.com; © A_Lesik/Shutterstock.com; © MegaShabanov/Shutterstock.com; © Groundback Atelier/Shutterstock.com; © saki80/Shutterstock.com

45th Parallel Press is an imprint of Cherry Lake Publishing.

Library of Congress Cataloging-in-Publication Data

Names: Loh-Hagan, Virginia, author. | Loh-Hagan, Virginia. History uncut.
Title: The real Albert Einstein / by Virginia Loh-Hagan.
Other titles: Albert Einstein
Description: Ann Arbor, MI : Cherry Lake Publishing, [2018] | Series: History uncut | Audience: Grades 7 to 8. | Includes bibliographical references and index.
Identifiers: LCCN 2018004560| ISBN 9781534129535 (hardcover) | ISBN 9781534132733 (pbk.) | ISBN 9781534131231 (pdf) | ISBN 9781534134430 (hosted ebook)
Subjects: LCSH: Einstein, Albert, 1879-1955—Juvenile literature. | Physicists—Biography—Juvenile literature.
Classification: LCC QC16.E5 L64 2018 | DDC 530.092 [B] —dc23
LC record available at https://lccn.loc.gov/2018004560

Cherry Lake Publishing would like to acknowledge the work of The Partnership for 21st Century Skills. Please visit www.p21.org for more information.

Printed in the United States of America
Corporate Graphics

Table of Contents

CHAPTER 1

Albert Einstein
The Story You Know

Albert Einstein was a scientist. He's most famous for his theories of relativity. Theories are ideas. They're scientific explanations. Relativity is how things are connected. Einstein explained how space relates to time. He also created the world's most famous equation. He showed how mass and energy were the same.

Einstein was a genius. Genius means a really smart person. He won the Nobel Prize. This is the highest honor in science. Einstein wrote over 300 science papers. He changed how people think. His ideas changed modern science.

But Einstein was more than just a scientist. There's much more to his story…

Einstein gave speeches. He traveled around the world.

CHAPTER 2

Special from Birth

Einstein was born in Germany. He was born on March 14, 1879. He was born with a big head. His head was a weird shape. His parents were worried about him. But his head changed. It became normal.

Einstein had speech problems. He didn't start talking until after most kids. He whispered words to himself. Then, he said them aloud. People did not think he was smart.

He didn't like school. He didn't listen to his teachers. He skipped classes. But he liked learning. He liked questioning. He was a **prodigy**. A prodigy is a young person with extraordinary talents. Einstein mastered hard math problems by age 15. He wrote his first science paper at age 16.

Einstein liked memorizing things.

SETTING THE WORLD STAGE
1879

> Frédéric Auguste Bartholdi was a French sculptor. He designed the Statue of Liberty. In 1879, he got a patent for his design. Patents are rights to ownership. The statue was gifted to the United States.

> Belva Ann Lockwood was a lawyer. She fought for women's rights. She pushed for new laws. She did this for 5 years. In 1879, President Rutherford B. Hayes signed a law. The law let female lawyers practice in federal court. Lockwood was the first woman to argue a case in the U.S. Supreme Court. She was the second woman to run for U.S. president.

> Thomas Edison was an inventor. In 1879, he invented a working electric light. He was the father of the lightbulb. He improved other designs. His light lasted longer. It needed less power. Edison built a system of power stations. These stations sent electricity to the lightbulbs. This spread the use of electric power.

Einstein learned to wonder. He was a curious child. His father showed him a **compass**. A compass is a tool. It shows direction. It has a needle that points north. Einstein was 5 years old. He wanted to figure out how it worked. He became interested in science.

At age 12, Einstein read a book. The book was about geometry. It inspired him. Max Talmey was a mentor. He ate dinner at the Einstein house. He talked about math. He talked about philosophy. This made Einstein think. He wondered about light beams. This led to his great ideas.

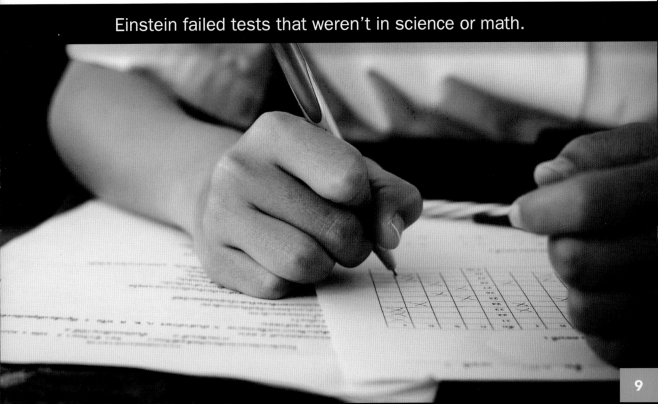

Einstein failed tests that weren't in science or math.

CHAPTER 3

Supporting the Bomb

Einstein didn't like Nazi Germany. His family was Jewish. Jewish people were treated very badly. They were taken from their homes. They were killed. Their rights were taken away.

The United States fought in World War II (WWII). It fought against Germany. Franklin D. Roosevelt was the U.S. president. Einstein wrote him letters. He learned Germany was working on a bomb. He told President Roosevelt about this. He said the United States should also make this bomb. He didn't believe in war. But he didn't want Germany to win.

His letters led to the Manhattan Project. This was top secret. Its goal was to make the **atom bomb**. The project started in Manhattan, New York.

World War II took place from 1939 to 1945.

Einstein didn't work on the bomb. He didn't have the **security clearance**. This means he didn't have top-secret status. But his ideas were used to build the bomb. Atom bombs are powerful. They release a lot of energy. They cause big explosions. They destroy cities. They kill people.

The project was successful. The United States used the atom bomb in war. It was the only country to do so. Einstein said, "I made one great mistake in my life—when I signed the letter to President Roosevelt recommending that atom bombs be made. But there was some justification—the danger that the Germans would make them."

What might have happened if the Nazis had won WWII?

All in the Family

Maria Einstein was Einstein's sister. She was called Maja. She was born on November 18, 1881. She was 2 years younger than Einstein. She was young Einstein's only friend. She even looked like him. She went to the University of Bern. She was a pianist. Maja married Paul Winteler. Winteler was a lawyer. Einstein studied under Winteler's father. Maja and Winteler lived in Italy. They hosted artists. They hosted thinkers. Italy was becoming anti-Jewish. It wasn't safe for Maja. Winteler was sick. He couldn't travel. Maja had to leave him behind. She planned on returning to him after the war. This never happened. She moved to the United States. She lived with Einstein. She got sick in 1946. She died in 1951.

"Learn from yesterday. Live for today. Hope for tomorrow. The important thing is not to stop questioning." — Albert Einstein

CHAPTER 4

Mad Scientist

Einstein did many strange things. He liked to shock people. There are many stories about him. First, he once ate a grasshopper. He picked it off the floor. He popped it in his mouth. Second, he picked up cigarette butts off the floor. He smoked them. Third, he didn't wear socks. He hated having his feet covered. He hated fixing sock holes. He saved time by not wearing them.

He didn't like **grooming**. Grooming is taking care of one's body. He had wild hair. He didn't like taking showers. He smelled. He didn't like getting dressed up. He wore a shirt. He wore baggy pants. He used a rope as a belt. He wore sandals.

Einstein liked sailing. But he didn't know how to swim.

THAT
Happened?!?

Albert Einstein went to Japan. He did this in 1922. He was famous at this time. He stayed at the Imperial Hotel in Tokyo. He tipped the hotel worker. He didn't give him cash. He gave him 2 notes. He said they'd be worth more than spare change. Both notes were signed and dated. The notes became known as "Einstein's Theory of Happiness." The first note was written on hotel paper. Einstein had written, "A calm and modest life brings more happiness than the pursuit of success combined with constant restlessness." That note was sold at auction. Auction is an event that sells things. The note was sold for over $1.5 million. It was the highest-priced document. There was another note. That note was written on blank scrap paper. It was sold for over $200,000. Einstein had written, "Where there's a will, there's a way."

"I have no special talents. I am only passionately curious."
— Albert Einstein

Einstein had many ideas. He was an inventor. This interest started when he was young. After he finished school, he had a hard time finding a teaching job. So, he worked in a patent office. He reviewed forms. This was the best job for him. He did his job quickly. So, he had time. He did other things. He studied. He wrote papers. He invented. He filed over 50 patents himself.

He designed an interesting shirt. The shirt changed sizes. It had two sets of buttons. Einstein could wear it when he was fat. He could wear it when he was skinny. He designed a camera. He designed a fridge. He designed a hearing aid.

A patent office has a lot of paperwork that needs to be done.

CHAPTER 5

Love and Marriages

Einstein was married twice. His first wife was Mileva Marić. Einstein's parents didn't like her. She was older. She wasn't Jewish.

Einstein and Marić met at school. Marić studied math. She and Einstein studied together. Some people think she helped write his papers. But there's no proof of that.

Their marriage lasted 16 years. They had 2 sons. Some people say they also had a daughter. The daughter's name was Leiserl. She was born before they were married. She died or disappeared.

Mileva Marić was the only woman in the math and science programs.

Einstein wasn't happy. He didn't treat Marić well. He had other lovers. He gave Marić rules. She had to clean the house. She had to feed him. She couldn't connect herself with him in public.

He started dating Elsa Einstein. She and Einstein grew up together. They were cousins. Their mothers were sisters. Their fathers were first cousins. Elsa became his second wife. She took care of Einstein. She nursed him when he was sick. She managed his business. She kept fans away.

Einstein still cheated on her. He had many lovers. Elsa was married to another man before Einstein. She had 3 children with him. Some people say Einstein fell in love with Elsa's daughter.

Einstein and Elsa moved to the United States together.

Bad Blood

Philipp Lenard was a scientist. He was born in 1862. He was a German. He worked on x-rays. He worked on atomic theory. He got a Nobel Prize in physics. Einstein had called him a genius. At first, he and Einstein were friends. But that changed. Lenard became a German nationalist. He didn't like Jewish people. He supported Adolf Hitler. He fought with Einstein. There was a big conference in 1920. Lenard said many bad things about Einstein. He said, "Just because a goat is born in a stable does not make him a noble thoroughbred." He wrote a book about great men in science. He didn't include Einstein. He thought Einstein stole his idea. He was jealous of Einstein. He said Einstein's theories were "Jewish fraud." Fraud means a trick.

"Any man who reads too much and uses his own brain too little falls into lazy habits of thinking." — Albert Einstein

CHAPTER 6

Lover of Music

Einstein said, "If I were not a physicist, I would probably be a musician. I often think in music. I live my daydreams in music. I see my life in terms of music . . . I do know that I get most joy in life out of my violin."

Einstein's mother played piano. She taught Einstein. She also gave him a violin. Einstein started at a young age. At first, he was better at piano. He also didn't like his violin lessons. Then, he heard Mozart's violin music. Mozart was a famous musician. Einstein was 13 years old. He fell in love with Mozart's music. He was inspired. He practiced more.

Einstein didn't like doing music drills.
He threw a chair at his violin teacher.

Music was part of his life. It helped him think better. Einstein played it when he was stuck. Playing gave him a new way of seeing things. He was able to solve problems. Playing violin also calmed him. His mind was always working. Music slowed him down. It gave him peace.

He played his whole life. He played with others. He performed for friends. Later in life, he walked around with his violin. He'd play and watch birds. Some say he was moved to tears. He brought a violin with him everywhere. He named his violin. He called it Lina. This was short for "violin."

◀ Elsa heard him play Mozart on his violin.
She fell in love with him.

CHAPTER 7

Wanted, Even in Death

Einstein supported peace. He didn't support war. He fought for civil rights. He spoke out against unfairness. He rejected Nazi Germany. But he was German. This made the **FBI** nervous. The FBI is a government agency. It investigates the breaking of laws.

The FBI thought he was a spy. **Agents** work for the FBI. They secretly watched him. They did this for over 22 years. They tracked everything he did. They listened to his phone calls. They read his mail. They looked at his trash. They watched him until he died. Some people thought he was building a death ray. Einstein's FBI file was almost 1,500 pages long.

Einstein got death threats.

Explained by
SCIENCE

Scientists think Einstein's IQ is between 160 and 190. IQ stands for "intelligence quotient." This is a measure of smartness. Scores above 140 are "genius" level. Playing violin helped Einstein. He used all his brain power. He combined logic and creativity. Scientists think musical training changes brains. It makes people smarter. It improves memory. It improves reasoning. It improves math skills. It improves literacy skills. It improves focus. It reduces stress. It makes people more alert. It slows the decline of old age. It keeps people smart as they age. Musicians use all their senses. They practice all the time.

"The true sign of intelligence is not knowledge but imagination."
— Albert Einstein

Einstein died on April 18, 1955. He didn't want doctors to save him. He said, "I have done my share. It is time to go." He died at age 76. He didn't want his brain or body to be studied. He wanted to be **cremated**. Cremated means to be burned to ashes. Einstein wanted his ashes scattered in secret places.

But his brain was removed. It was taken without permission. Scientists wanted to save it. They wanted to study it. They wanted to see why he was so smart. They took many pictures. They cut it into different pieces.

Einstein's genius will never be forgotten.

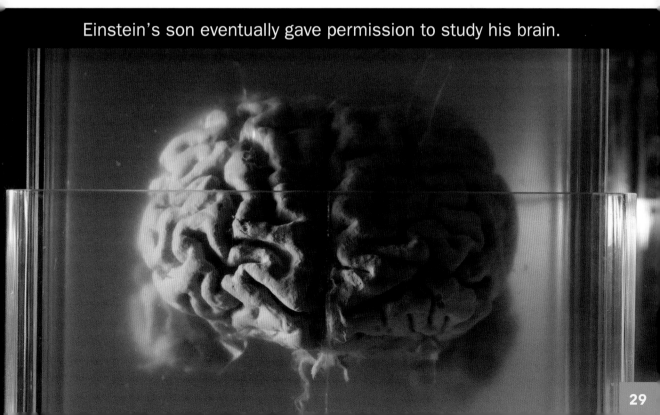

Einstein's son eventually gave permission to study his brain.

Timeline

1879 Einstein was born. His parents were Hermann and Pauline.

1885 Einstein went to a Catholic school. He learned about the Jewish religion at home. He started violin lessons.

1894 Einstein moved to Milan, Italy.

1896 Einstein renounced his German citizenship. He wanted to avoid joining the military.

1901 Einstein became a Swiss citizen.

1902 Einstein worked in the patent office. He did this for about 7 years.

1902 Einstein started a discussion group. He invited his university friends. The group was called the Olympia Academy. They read. They talked about science and philosophy.

1903 Einstein married Mileva Marić.

1904 Einstein's first son was born. His name was Hans Albert.

1905 Einstein got his doctorate. He wrote a lot of science papers. This was called his "miracle year."

1910 Einstein's second son was born. His name was Eduard. Eduard had a breakdown at age 20.

1919 Einstein's theory is confirmed. There was a solar eclipse. Scientists were able to prove Einstein's theory. He became famous.

1919 Einstein divorced Marić. He promised to pay her every year. He used the money he'd get from the Nobel Prize.

1921 Einstein visited the United States. This was his first visit. He was raising money for the Hebrew University in Jerusalem.

1922 Einstein won the Nobel Prize.

1933 Einstein announced he wouldn't return to Germany. This was after the Nazis took over Germany.

1933 Einstein moved to the United States.

1940 Einstein became a U.S. citizen.

1952 Einstein declined the presidency of Israel.

1955 Einstein died. His ashes were scattered secretly and papers were sent to the Hebrew University.

Consider This!

Take a Position! Einstein was treated like a rock star. He had many fans. He said, "No living person deserves this sort of reception." Do you think he should be celebrated like a rock star? Argue your point with reasons and evidence.

Say What? Read the 45th Parallel Press book about Marie Curie. How are Einstein and Curie connected? Compare them. Explain how they're the same. Explain how they're different.

Think About It! Being different is good. People's strange habits are what make them special. Einstein had many strange habits. Think about your own strange habits. Make a list. Pick the strangest habit. What is it? Why do you do this? Do other people have this habit?

Learn More

Krull, Kathleen, and Boris Kulikov (illust.). *Albert Einstein*. New York: Viking, 2015.

Pohlen, Jerome. *Albert Einstein and Relativity for Kids: His Life and Ideas with 21 Activities and Thought Experiments*. Chicago: Chicago Review Press, 2012.

Romero, Libby. *Albert Einstein*. Washington, DC: National Geographic, 2016.

Glossary

agents (AY-juhnts) people who work for an agency

atom bomb (AT-uhm BAHM) powerful bomb that releases a lot of energy, causing big explosions

compass (KUHM-puhs) a tool used for navigation or orientation

cremated (KREE-mate-id) to be burned until a body becomes ashes

FBI (EF BEE EYE) Federal Bureau of Investigation, a government agency that investigates the violations of federal laws

genius (JEEN-yuhs) extraordinary intelligence

grooming (GROOM-ing) the process of taking care of oneself by washing, dressing, etc.

Nobel Prize (NO-behl PRIZE) an award that goes to people who do important work in science and art or toward peace; they are given out every year

prodigy (PRAH-dih-jee) a young person with extraordinary talents or gifts

relativity (rel-uh-TIV-ih-tee) the state of being relative or connected

security clearance (sih-KYOOR-ih-tee KLEER-uhns) having the appropriate background that enables one to have access to top-secret information

theories (THEER-eez) ideas; scientific explanations

Index

About the Author

Dr. Virginia Loh-Hagan is an author, university professor, former classroom teacher, and curriculum designer. Like Einstein, she doesn't like to waste time grooming. She lives in San Diego with her very tall husband and very naughty dogs. To learn more about her, visit www.virginialoh.com.